Original title:
Frost-Covered Dreams

Copyright © 2024 Swan Charm
All rights reserved.

Author: Aron Pilviste
ISBN HARDBACK: 978-9916-79-480-7
ISBN PAPERBACK: 978-9916-79-481 4
ISBN EBOOK: 978-9916-79-482-1

The Dream Weaver's Winter Web

In a world of frost and chill,
The weaver spins with gentle skill.
Threads of silver, light as air,
Binding dreams with tender care.

Underneath the moon's soft gaze,
Whispers float in snowy haze.
Each design a secret passed,
Held in velvet, futures cast.

A tapestry of hopes and fears,
Woven softly, through the years.
In the night, the patterns swell,
Silent stories, hearts can tell.

With each flicker of the stars,
The weaver's dance plays near and far.
A winter's mist begins to rise,
Crafting dreams beneath cold skies.

So in this web of soft delight,
Find the warmth within the night.
Embrace the chill, let spirits soar,
For the weaver's gift is evermore.

Crystal Dreams in the Twilight Glow

Twilight whispers through the trees,
Carrying dreams upon the breeze.
Crystals form in sharp delight,
Glistening under fading light.

Each flake dances, a fleeting grace,
Softly landing, a fleeting trace.
In this moment, time stands still,
Breath of magic, heartbeats thrill.

Gentle hues of purple rise,
Painting shadows in the skies.
Within the glow, reflections beam,
Awakening our hidden dream.

Echoes of a world away,
Cradle hopes in soft array.
Every glimmer tells a tale,
Of whispered secrets in the pale.

As night enfolds the land in care,
Crystal dreams float through the air.
In this twilight's tender song,
We find the place where we belong.

Veils of Snowy Illusions

Softly falls the whispering snow,
Veiling all in a gentle glow.
Each flake drifts with quiet ease,
Wrapping earth in winter's tease.

Beneath the drifts, the world holds tight,
Secrets cloaked in purest white.
Time slows down, we pause to see,
What lies hidden, yet to be.

Mirrored skies and frosted trees,
All around, a silent freeze.
Illusions dance on winter's breath,
Painting paths where dreams find death.

In this realm of chilly grace,
Nature wears a fragile face.
Within the quiet, mysteries weave,
In snowy veils, we dare believe.

A gentle sigh, a fleeting thought,
In every storm, we find what's sought.
These illusions, soft and bright,
Lead us further into night.

A Dance with Winter's Breath

The winter wind begins to play,
A dance of chill, night turns to day.
Frosty fingers touch the ground,
In this rhythm, beauty's found.

With every gust, the landscape sways,
Whispers echo through the bays.
Nature twirls in frosty robes,
As icy notes sing from the globes.

Shadows weave beneath the light,
Crisp and clear, a wondrous sight.
In this symphony of cold,
Stories of the brave unfold.

Each step taken, heartbeats sing,
Odes to joy the season brings.
Let the breath of winter flow,
In this dance, our spirits grow.

As stars above begin to gleam,
Join the dance, embrace the dream.
For in this season's fleeting flight,
We find our warmth in winter's night.

Ethereal Chill in the Air

A whisper through the trees,
Cool breath on weary skin,
Beneath the twilight's gaze,
The dusk begins to spin.

Stars begin to flicker,
In the deepening blue,
A hush envelops all,
As night begins anew.

Each leaf a silver tremor,
Each shadow drawn in light,
The world breathes softly,
In the embrace of night.

A chill that wraps the soul,
In quiet, soft refrain,
Echoes of forgotten,
In the chill, yet remain.

The Quietude of Winter's Heart

Snowflakes drift like whispers,
Kissing the world so white,
Every branch adorned softly,
In the gentle light.

The valley holds its breath,
In a blanket of peace,
Nature still, serene,
In winter's sweet release.

Time drips like melting icicles,
In this timeless embrace,
Each moment stretched and endless,
In the frozen space.

The firewood crackles low,
A dance of warmth and flame,
While outside, silent night,
Calls winter by its name.

In the stillness, we find,
A solace deep and pure,
In the quietude of hearts,
The winter's heart is sure.

Muffled Secrets Beneath Snow

Beneath the frosty blanket,
Whispers softly lie,
Secrets held in stillness,
As time drifts slowly by.

Footsteps vanish gently,
In the soft, pale white,
While nature's hand conceals
All the dreams of night.

Roots and echoes hidden,
Under layers of frost,
A tale of silent slumber,
In the cold, not lost.

The world, a quiet canvas,
Painted in hushed tones,
Where echoes of the summer,
Lie wrapped in gentle moans.

As dawn unveils the morning,
The secrets start to stir,
Yet muffled by the snow,
Their whispers softly purr.

Moonlit Hues on a Shivering Canvas

Underneath the pale moonlight,
A world begins to glow,
With hues of silver whispers,
And shadows soft and low.

Each branch a silhouette,
Against the starlit sky,
The night wraps all in wonder,
As time begins to fly.

Crystals dance on rooftops,
A sparkling display,
While dreams paint the horizon,
In the dawning gray.

The frost, a fleeting artist,
On nature's tender skin,
Her colors ever-changing,
As she breathes deep within.

In moonlit hues, we wander,
On this shivering canvas bare,
Finding beauty in the nocturne,
In the whispers of the air.

Whispers of Winter's Veil

Snowflakes dance in soft silence,
Blanketing all with a hush.
The bare branches wear their diamonds,
Cradling the cold's tender brush.

Frosted whispers fill the air,
Tales of winter, old and wise.
In the glow of candle's glare,
Dreams awaken beneath the skies.

Crisp breaths in the quiet night,
Stars twinkle like frosty breath.
Nature sighs in silver light,
Embracing the stillness of death.

Icicles hang like crystal chimes,
Glistening faintly in the glow.
Every moment, frozen times,
In the heart of winter's show.

Through the woods, a path unfolds,
Footsteps muffled, soft and slow.
Whispers of stories yet untold,
Winter's magic begins to flow.

Shimmering Slumber

Softly falls the tranquil snow,
A blanket pure, a gentle grace.
Moonlight glimmers, a silver show,
As dreams take flight in quiet space.

Whispers wrap the world in peace,
Stars twinkle through the evening mist.
Time's slow flow gives souls release,
In shimmering slumber, none are missed.

Echoes of laughter in the night,
Winds carry tales from days of yore.
Each flake a wish, a pure delight,
In slumber's arms, we all explore.

Beneath the sky, the earth is still,
A canvas painted white and bright.
Guarded by peace, a tender thrill,
In shimmering dreams, we find our light.

As dawn emerges, soft and new,
The world awakens from its dream.
With every hue, a lovely view,
In shimmering slumber, hearts will gleam.

Icy Breath of Night

Night descends with icy breath,
Chilling whispers through the trees.
Shadows creep, a dance with death,
In the moonlight's silver tease.

The world adorned in frosty lace,
Glimmers bright, yet feels so cold.
Nature holds a quiet grace,
Stories in the night unfold.

Stars reflect on frozen streams,
Glass-like surfaces that gleam.
In the dark, the heart still beams,
Weaving through this silent dream.

Cold winds sigh, a lullaby,
As velvet night wraps close and tight.
In the stillness, time drifts by,
Beneath the watch of shimmering light.

Icy breath of night persists,
Kissing the earth with frosty air.
Each whisper grows, as nature twists,
In eternal dance, our minds ensnare.

Glacial Reveries

In the hush of frozen lands,
Dreams unfold like melting streams.
Whispers flow from icy hands,
Painting all with glacial dreams.

Mountains rise like ancient guards,
Standing tall against the chill.
Nature's peace, a world of shards,
In quiet reverie, time stands still.

Tender glows from distant lights,
Guide the weary through the night.
Every star, a thousand sights,
Sparkling in their frosty flight.

Voices echo on the breeze,
Secrets held by frost and fire.
In this realm of silent pleas,
Hope rejoices, dreams aspire.

Glacial reveries take hold,
Embracing hearts with icy grace.
In the quiet, truths unfold,
Winter's charm, our warm embrace.

A Symphony of Winter's Whispers

Snowflakes dance upon the breeze,
Gentle whispers, nature's tease.
Trees stand tall in winter's white,
Silent song beneath the night.

Moonlight glimmers on the ground,
A serene hush, all around.
Stars are glistening, oh so bright,
Painting dreams in soft twilight.

Frosty breath fills the chilly air,
Icicles hang with jeweled flair.
Crackling fires warm the soul,
In this season, we feel whole.

Windswept fields stretch far and wide,
Nature's beauty, winter's pride.
Harmony in every flake,
A melody that we awake.

As we gather, hearts align,
In this moment, all divine.
Whispers of the season's grace,
In winter's symphony, we find our place.

Glimpses of Silvered Slumber

Silver mist cloaks the sleeping earth,
Softly whispering of rebirth.
Fields of frost, a sparkling sight,
Dreaming deeply through the night.

Moon's embrace brings a tranquil glow,
Silent shadows dance below.
Nature rests, the world in pause,
A gentle peace without a cause.

Winter's breath, a lullaby,
Crystals twinkle in the sky.
Every step, a muffled sound,
In this stillness, joy is found.

Stars peek through the velvet dark,
Glimmers twirl, a fleeting spark.
Underneath, the world lies still,
Anticipation, time will fill.

When the sun begins to rise,
Colors bloom, no more disguise.
Yet in dreams, the silver gleams,
A soft blanket, wrapped in dreams.

Breaths of Ice and Fire

Flickering flames in the hearth's embrace,
Dance with shadows, a warm, bright space.
Outside, the world is crisp and cold,
A tale of two seasons, daring and bold.

Winter's breath forms a frosty veil,
While embers glow and winds set sail.
Ice crystals seek the sun's soft kiss,
In this contrast, we find our bliss.

Chill of night meets warmth within,
Echoes of laughter, where we begin.
Fireflies dance through the midnight air,
Two forces merge, beyond compare.

Moments shared near the glowing light,
Whispers and dreams take flight at night.
In this balance, we find our way,
Breaths of ice and fire will stay.

Seasons shift in a timeless dance,
In harmony, we take our chance.
A tapestry woven, stark yet bright,
Breaths unite in fading light.

Memories Etched in Frost

Frosty mornings greet the dawn,
Whispers of voices, memories drawn.
Each crystal tells a tale of old,
A world of wonders, secrets told.

Footsteps crunch upon the ground,
In frozen paths, lost love is found.
Every breath leaves a fleeting trace,
In winter's grasp, time slows its pace.

Shimmers dance on window panes,
Through the glass, a portrait remains.
Of laughter shared and dreams once held,
In silent echoes, our hearts compelled.

With each snowfall, the past rewinds,
Wisps of joy in frosted finds.
Nature's canvas, a gentle frost,
In every moment, we find what's lost.

Yet as the thaw begins to creep,
Memories are ours to keep.
In the warmth that follows frost,
In time's embrace, we count the cost.

Snapshots of Serenity in Ice

Crystal whispers in the air,
Nature's art beyond compare,
Silent moments, frozen still,
Time holds breath, a muted thrill.

Glistening branches, softly sway,
Underneath the sky's gray sway,
Dreamy patterns, shimmering light,
Whispers of the coldest night.

Mirror lakes reflect the stars,
Fallen snowflakes, tiny shards,
Distant echoes, soft and clear,
In the silence, peace draws near.

Frosted windows, hidden views,
Nature paints with crystal hues,
Each snapshot, a moment's grace,
Captured essence in this place.

Beneath blankets, dreams unfold,
Stories whispered, tales retold,
In this realm of icy bliss,
Serenity awaits with a kiss.

Frosted Prisms of the Night

In the silence, stars collide,
Frosted prisms, worlds abide,
Whispers linger on the breeze,
Underneath the ancient trees.

Moonbeams dance on frozen ground,
Magic lingers, all around,
Crystals shimmer, soft and bright,
Embers glow in the cold night.

The sky adorned in twinkling show,
Each star a dream, a gentle glow,
Nature's canvas, deep and wide,
In frosted moments, time won't hide.

Glistening shadows weave and sway,
Painting stories in the gray,
Frosted whispers, night's lament,
Moments captured, softly spent.

As dawn approaches, hues arise,
Promising life 'neath winter skies,
Frosted prisms, fleeting light,
Guardians of the tranquil night.

Silhouettes Under a Glassy Dream

In the twilight, shapes define,
Silhouettes, the stars align,
Glassy dreams, reflections form,
Nature's beauty, calm and warm.

Delicate shadows whisper low,
Underneath the night's soft glow,
Moving gracefully in the air,
Each moment, a fleeting prayer.

Crystalline branches touch the sky,
While starlit echoes softly sigh,
Beneath the moon's watchful gaze,
Glassy dreams weave through the haze.

Every heartbeat, a tale confessed,
In the quiet, hearts find rest,
Underneath the veil of night,
Silhouettes, in silver light.

Together they dance, shadows blend,
In this dream, there's no end,
Whispers of the night abide,
In silhouettes, we confide.

Lullabies of the Frosted Woods

Softly sung under moon's embrace,
Lullabies, a gentle trace,
Frosted woods, where silence calls,
Nature's cradle, peace enthralls.

Whispers flow like melting snow,
Nurtured dreams in twilight's glow,
Every rustle, every sigh,
In the stillness, spirits fly.

Branches shiver, tales unfold,
In the chill, hearts warm and bold,
Wrapped in night's tender hold,
The wood sings of love untold.

Snowflakes drift, a soft ballet,
Guiding thoughts on winter's way,
Lullabies in hushed refrain,
Echo through the frost-kissed plain.

In the dark, a lullaby's balm,
Cradles dreams with whispered calm,
The frosted woods, a sacred sphere,
Where hearts find rest, the world unclear.

When Stars Glimmer like Ice

In the quiet of night, they gleam,
Whispers of dreams, like a silver stream.
Each twinkle a promise, a wish made true,
Frozen in time, like morning dew.

They shimmer and dance in the vast unknown,
Painting the sky, a celestial throne.
With each blink, they light up the dark,
Guiding lost souls with their soft spark.

When shadows creep in, they stand so bold,
Tales of the cosmos, forever told.
A symphony sung in the still of the night,
When stars glimmer like ice, glowing bright.

Veins of Silver in Winter's Heart

Through the frost-kissed trees, whispers flow,
Veins of silver in the soft, white glow.
Nature's breath held in a frozen sigh,
Silent stories of the earth and sky.

Beneath the surface, life stirs and waits,
Wrapped in a blanket of winter's fates.
Every flake a tale, delicate and rare,
Adorned with jewels, beyond compare.

The chill in the air speaks secrets untold,
Of warmth to return, a promise of gold.
In the heart of the cold, still beats a fire,
Veins of silver whispering desire.

The Shivering Canvas of Night

A tapestry woven with threads of dark,
The shivering canvas awaits a spark.
Stars drip like paint, through the inky sea,
Crafting new worlds, wild and free.

Moonlight spills secrets on soft, silent ground,
Echoes of whispers that linger around.
Every shadow moves, a dance in the gloom,
Breathing life into the stillness of doom.

Dreams are painted where night softly bleeds,
A gallery rich with humanity's needs.
In this vast expanse, we find our place,
The shivering canvas holds our trace.

Awakening Beneath the Snow's Weight

Under the blanket, the earth holds its breath,
Awakening slowly from whispers of death.
Seeds dream below in their cozy retreat,
Waiting for warmth to mark their defeat.

Each layer of snow is a soft lullaby,
Covering life as it patiently lies.
In silence, it stirs, ready to break free,
From the grip of the cold, to bask in the spree.

When spring's gentle touch brushes the ground,
The promise of life will echo around.
Awakening beneath the snow's heavy weight,
Nature will flourish, a dance to create.

Suspended in Cold Light

Underneath the pale moon glow,
Shadows dance, both high and low.
Breath of winter, crisp and clear,
Whispers soft, as night draws near.

Stars above like frozen tears,
Time stands still, yet comes the years.
In this realm of quiet grace,
Memories linger, thoughts embrace.

A world wrapped in silver sheen,
Echoes of what might have been.
In the silence, hearts unite,
Suspended in the cold light.

Frosted dreams on window panes,
Elusive touch of frozen chains.
Yearnings trapped in icy flow,
Fading whispers, come and go.

With every breath, the stillness grows,
In the darkness, beauty glows.
Here in twilight's gentle hold,
Secrets shared, unspoken, bold.

Frostbitten Memories

Footprints lead to places lost,
Eager hearts now count the cost.
Time has stolen warmth away,
Leaving echoes, turned to gray.

Frostbitten dreams and laughter freeze,
Moments captured, scattered leaves.
In the chill, I hear your voice,
Calling softly, I rejoice.

Bitter winds that softly brush,
Stir the past in silent hush.
Every memory, a fragile spark,
Illuminates the endless dark.

Shadows whisper, shadows sigh,
As the seasons drift and fly.
Frozen kisses, moments shared,
In the quiet, love declared.

Through the frost, I see it clear,
Warmth still lives, though you are near.
In the heart, the chill decays,
Frostbitten, yet love stays.

Chill of the Silent Dawn

Morning breaks with muted light,
Crisp and sharp, the world feels right.
Frost clings to the vacant trees,
Nature stirs with gentle ease.

Whispers in the chilly air,
Promises of warmth laid bare.
Golden rays begin to weave,
Cloaks of warmth that soon retrieve.

Silent footsteps on the ground,
Nature listens, no sound found.
Through the glades, the breath of dawn,
Chill retreats, the night is gone.

Soon, the colors will ignite,
Waking dreams from frozen night.
Yet in the stillness, time records,
Chill of dawn, the heart restores.

In the light, a new day stirs,
Nature hums soft melodies,
Carried forth by wind's embrace,
Chill retreats, beneath the grace.

Ethereal Echoes in Ice

Glaciers whisper ancient tales,
Time's embrace, the silence pales.
Frozen hearts beat soft and low,
Echoes linger, ebb and flow.

Chill of night, the silence sings,
Melodies of frost, cold wings.
Each breath released, a crystal shard,
Beauty stark, yet ever hard.

In the twilight, shadows crawl,
Nature's canvas, pure and tall.
Fractured light reflects the skies,
Within the ice, a truth lies.

Ethereal dreams weave through the white,
Caught in stillness, wrapped in light.
Whispers carried on the breeze,
Frozen moments, time's reprise.

In this space, the world fades slow,
Ethereal echoes in the snow.
Here, the spirit finds its flight,
In the depths of cold, pure light.

Twilight's Wintry Embrace

In the hush, the snowflakes twirl,
Beneath a sky of indigo swirl.
Shadows dance with fading light,
Whispers of the coming night.

Trees wrapped in silver lace,
Stand guard in this quiet space.
Stars peek through the frosty veil,
Nature's soft, enchanting tale.

A chill that bites, yet feels so sweet,
With every footstep, the ground's heartbeat.
Footprints linger, secrets told,
In twilight's charm, the world turns gold.

A gentle breeze, a breath divine,
Casts a magic, so sublime.
Embracing winter's soft caress,
In this moment, we find peace.

As day gives in, horizons fade,
In twilight's arms, our fears unmade.
This beautiful, tranquil space,
Sweet winter's wintry embrace.

A Canvas of White Dreams

Upon the ground, a quilt of white,
Blankets the earth in pure delight.
A canvas stretched, untouched, serene,
Where dreams float soft, so light, unseen.

Above, the sky is painted blue,
A cobalt sweep with clouds anew.
Each breath we take, a cloud of mist,
In this pure realm, the world exists.

Footprints lead on paths anew,
Sketching tales of me and you.
Laughter bubbles, joy unchained,
In this white dream, we all remain.

Icicles hang like crystal tears,
Adorning branches through the years.
Nature's art, a wondrous sight,
Bringing warmth to winter's bite.

With every glance, a magic found,
A tranquil heart, a joyful sound.
In the hush of snow's embrace,
A canvas of dreams, pure and chaste.

Tranquil Waters of Ice and Light

In the stillness, reflections gleam,
Wrapped in winter's gentle dream.
Silhouette of trees oblique,
Icy waters, soft and sleek.

Moonlight dances on the pond,
Liquid silver stretched beyond.
Where whispers echo, soft and sweet,
Nature's lullaby, pure and fleet.

Misty breaths rise into the air,
A portrait drawn with utmost care.
Frozen patterns, intricate, fine,
A transient beauty, so divine.

Rays of sunbreak softly weave,
Through branches bare, a gentle reprieve.
In the calm, our spirits lift,
A moment cherished, a priceless gift.

Here in silence, hearts take flight,
Tranquil waters, both ice and light.
Nature's canvas quietly shows,
The peace that only winter knows.

Nightfall's Frosted Whimsy

As twilight falls, the world awakes,
In frosted coats, the silence shakes.
Stars twinkle in the dusky glow,
While the moon cradles dreams below.

Snowflakes waltz on whispers cool,
Painting dreams, the night's sweet jewel.
In shadows deep, the magic stirs,
As laughter dances, all that blurs.

The winds carry tales from afar,
Of ancient woods and twilight star.
A frozen breath, a sigh of light,
In nightfall's whimsy, pure delight.

Beneath the trees, the secrets hide,
Where creatures dwell and dreams abide.
In the silence, sweet stories spring,
As night unfolds her delicate wing.

With every glance, a spark is caught,
In frosted whimsy, we are wrought.
Together, under the vast, dark dome,
In nightfall's arms, we find our home.

Silent Crystals of the Night

Beneath the moon, the crystals gleam,
A whispering hush, a distant dream.
Stars sparkle softly in the deep,
Guarding secrets that they keep.

Frosty breath upon the air,
Echoing tales of winter's care.
Each flake dances, pure delight,
Silent crystals of the night.

Shadows shimmer in silvery hue,
As night unfolds its chilling view.
Branches sway, adorned in frost,
In this beauty, never lost.

The world sleeps under a starry veil,
Whispers of magic tell the tale.
Nature's wonders, pure and bright,
Forever captured in the night.

With each breath, the cold ignites,
A symphony of tranquil sights.
In stillness, we find true delight,
In the glow of silent night.

Lullabies of the North Wind

The north wind sings a gentle tune,
Underneath the pale moon's broom.
Snowflakes flutter, soft and light,
Lullabies of the winter night.

Whispers weave through barren trees,
Carrying secrets on the breeze.
Cosmic dances in the sky,
As stars twinkle and softly sigh.

Crisp air fills the longing heart,
Each note a warming work of art.
Wrapped in wool, we find our peace,
In winter's song, our souls release.

Fires crackle, shadows play,
As dreams drift softly far away.
The north wind sings in hushed delight,
Lullabies of the endless night.

Through darkened voids, we feel the pull,
These melodies, soft and full.
In every sigh, our spirits soar,
With lullabies, forevermore.

Enchanted by the Hibernal Light

Softly glows the hibernal light,
Casting shadows, pure and bright.
Crystals sparkling on the ground,
In every glance, magic found.

Frozen whispers fill the air,
Enchanting dreams beyond compare.
Brittle branches glisten, sway,
As dusk invites the night to play.

The world is draped in icy lace,
Winter's touch, a warm embrace.
In this wonder, hearts take flight,
Enchanted by the hibernal light.

Time stands still in this sacred space,
Each moment cherished at a pace.
Stillness offers gifts untold,
Stories of the brave and bold.

In quietude, the spirit roams,
Finding solace, creating homes.
With every shimmer, love ignites,
In the magic of hibernal nights.

Surrender to the Winter's Grace

In the stillness, find your peace,
Surrender deep, let worries cease.
Winter's grace that blankets low,
Softening hearts with gentle flow.

Each breath a dance with frosty air,
A moment's pause, a whispered prayer.
Through swirling snow, the silence calls,
In winter's arms, our spirit falls.

Amidst the white, we learn to roam,
Finding strength in nature's home.
Every flake a tale to trace,
A reminder of winter's grace.

With every sunset, shadows blend,
In twilight's glow, the day will mend.
As stars emerge, we find our space,
Surrendering to winter's grace.

In quiet moments, joy awakens,
In every breath, warmth is taken.
Embrace the chill, let spirit soar,
Surrender now, forevermore.

Ephemeral Snowflakes on Dreams

Softly they drift, a fleeting sight,
Each flake a whisper in the night.
They touch the earth, then melt away,
Leaving behind a silvery spray.

In the glow of the moon, they twirl,
Dancing dreams in a frosty swirl.
A moment's grace, a breath of air,
Ephemeral beauty, beyond compare.

Silent wishes on chilly breeze,
Fleeting glimpses among the trees.
Memories captured, briefly held,
In dreams where winter's magic swelled.

Their journey ends, but hearts will cling,
To the joys that fragile moments bring.
In the stillness, they find their rest,
Ephemeral dreams, forever blessed.

As dawn approaches, they fade away,
Yet in our hearts, they choose to stay.
A soft reminder of moments brief,
Snowflakes on dreams, a cherished belief.

In the Twilight of Frosted Wishes

In twilight's glow, the world is still,
Frosted wishes, a soft thrill.
Stars begin to sparkle bright,
As shadows dance in the fading light.

Snowflakes gather, a tender quilt,
Whispers of dreams that time has built.
They twinkle under a silvery sheen,
Frosted wishes, fragile and serene.

A wish upon a falling star,
In winter's heart, we've come so far.
Each frost-kissed breath, a hopeful sigh,
In this twilight where wishes lie.

The quiet hum of the night surrounds,
Echoing softly, as silence drowns.
In this moment, time stands still,
In the twilight's glow, we find our thrill.

Then morning comes with a soft embrace,
Frosted wishes leave not a trace.
But in our hearts, they softly gleam,
In the twilight of a winter's dream.

The Quietude of White Nightfall

As night descends, the world goes white,
Quietude blankets the fading light.
Snowflakes murmur with a gentle grace,
In this stillness, we find our place.

The air is crisp, a soothing balm,
Wrapped in winter's quiet calm.
Stars twinkle softly in the vast expanse,
In the quietude, we find our chance.

Each flake a story, unique and rare,
Whispers of dreams linger in the air.
With every breath, a moment divine,
In white nightfall's embrace, we align.

Underneath the moon's soft glow,
Nature pauses, the world slows.
In the quietude, hearts expand,
Finding solace in winter's hand.

As dawn approaches, the night will fade,
Yet memories of stillness will cascade.
In the quietude of white nightfall,
We hold the magic, we hold it all.

Diaphanous Dreams in Frigid Air

In the chill of night, dreams are spun,
Diaphanous whispers, two become one.
They float like mist on a tranquil stream,
In the frigid air, we're lost in dream.

With each gentle breath, they rise and swirl,
A dance of hopes, a snowy twirl.
Through frosted windows, our spirits soar,
Diaphanous dreams, forevermore.

Stars twinkle down with a knowing glow,
In each fleeting moment, we choose to grow.
Wrapped in winter's embrace so tight,
In frigid air, we find our light.

As dawn begins to break the spell,
Diaphanous dreams cast a shimmering shell.
Though fleeting, they leave a gentle trace,
In the heart's warm glow, they find their place.

So let us wander, hearts unconfined,
In dreams of winter, our souls aligned.
Together we rise, in frosty delight,
Chasing diaphanous dreams through the night.

A Basket of Icebound Daydreams

In a world where wishes freeze,
Whispers float on icy breeze.
Crystals form from thoughts unwound,
Nestled deep in dreams profound.

Frosted petals softly sigh,
Beneath the vast and starry sky.
Each glimmer holds a secret tale,
Frozen hopes that seldom fail.

Silent echoes dance in snow,
Starlit paths where dreamers go.
In a basket woven tight,
Daydreams glimmer, pure and bright.

When the dawn begins to break,
Shadows melt, and hearts awake.
A tapestry of light unfurls,
In the cradle of the worlds.

The icebound dreams paint skies anew,
With every twinkle, visions brew.
A journey through the crystal night,
Guided by the morning light.

Rime-Draped Reverie

On a canvas flecked with frost,
Echoes of the past embossed.
Rime-draped whispers softly gleam,
Unraveling the fragile dream.

A gentle touch of winter's breath,
Awakens life amidst the death.
With each breath, the silence calls,
As twilight softly wraps and falls.

In this haze, the spirits dance,
Caught within a frozen trance.
Draped in silver, cloaked in white,
Swirling visions take their flight.

Every flake a moment caught,
Fragments of a world forgot.
Through the stillness, colors blend,
In rime's embrace, we transcend.

Yet when the thaw begins to rise,
Morning breaks with dazzling skies.
Rime-draped paths, though transient, stay,
In the heart, they'll find their way.

Pearls of Frost in Cosmic Whispers

Beneath the cosmic twilight glow,
Pearls of frost on branches grow.
Gentle whispers in the night,
Speaking secrets wrapped in light.

Stars like diamonds, cold and bright,
Woven into winter's bite.
Dreams awaken, soft and clear,
In the quiet, we draw near.

Galaxies spin with tales to tell,
In the silence, where dreams dwell.
Frosted echoes drift and play,
Painting shadows on the way.

As the universe sighs and sways,
Magic lingers in the haze.
Each small pearl, a wish so dear,
In cosmic realms, our hopes appear.

With every night, a new design,
Frosted dreams that intertwine.
In the vastness, we find grace,
In the universe's embrace.

Beneath the Silver Layer

Underneath the silver veil,
Whispers ride on winter's gale.
Secrets tucked in snowflakes' sighs,
Hiding dreams where stillness lies.

Branches wear a crystal crown,
Softly sparkling in the town.
Every corner softly glows,
With the magic that it knows.

Footsteps crunch on frosty ground,
In the quiet, peace is found.
Beneath the layer, life does hum,
In nature's rhythm, we become.

Flakes descend like wishes made,
Painting paths that never fade.
Underneath the silver night,
Hearts awaken to the light.

In the twilight, shadows roam,
Crafting stories yet unknown.
Beneath the silver layer wide,
Hope and wonder now abide.

Dreams Adrift on Winter's Sea

Waves of white dance high,
Echoes of dreams set free.
Sailing on the cold sigh,
Beneath the moon's decree.

Guided by the starlight,
Whispers of the deep night.
Hopes adrift, taking flight,
In the chill, a soft light.

Frosted winds softly tease,
Carrying the night's ease.
Glimmers on icy seas,
Where visions find their keys.

Amidst the frozen drift,
A world of memory skinned,
Where silver shadows gift,
A touch of warmth within.

Night's embrace tightly binds,
Memories left behind.
In winter's hold, one finds,
The heart's unique designs.

The Art of Frosted Whispers

Silence speaks in the cold,
Whispers wrapped in white.
Each breath a tale retold,
In the still of the night.

Patterns drawn in the frost,
Nature's delicate hand.
Every moment embossed,
On crystal-like strands.

Hushed secrets twirl and spin,
Dancing in the pale glow.
Soft sighs beneath the skin,
Where only dreams can go.

A canvas of pure grace,
Framed by winter's design.
In each fleeting embrace,
Artistry divine.

Frosted whispers remain,
Tracing pathways unseen.
Echoes of summer's reign,
In winter's serene sheen.

Glaze of Twenty Below

A frigid kiss on skin,
Chilled laughter fills the air.
Tales of winter begin,
In the crystal glare.

Branches draped in white,
Crafted by icy breath.
Morning dawns with light,
Veiling all that is left.

Shadows stretching long,
Beneath the frosted sky.
Nature sings a song,
Of warmth that's drawing nigh.

Every step a crunch,
Echoes through the stillness.
Time feels like a punch,
On the edge of chillness.

In the glaze of the cold,
Magic weaves through the day.
Stories yet untold,
In winter's gentle sway.

Frozen Petals of Hope

Buds encased in the freeze,
Waiting for warmer hands.
Carried by winter's breeze,
They dream of sunlit lands.

Petals cloaked in frost,
Crystals upon each bloom.
In silence, they are lost,
Whispering in the gloom.

Yet beneath the white shroud,
Life stirs with quiet grace.
Hope rests in hearts unbowed,
Longing for spring's embrace.

Each layer tells a tale,
Of resilient desire.
Through the icicles' veil,
Burns a hidden fire.

Frozen petals will break,
In the sun's tender gaze.
Life's promise, they will take,
To burst forth in a blaze.

Echoes in the Winter Air

Whispers in the frosty night,
Silver stars shining bright,
Footprints crunch on frozen ground,
In silence, dreams abound.

Branches bare stand tall and proud,
Wrapped in mist, a shrouded crowd,
Echoes of a distant call,
Empty streets, and shadows fall.

A breath of cold, it lingers near,
Softest whispers, slight and clear,
Nature's song, a gentle hum,
In winter's grip, all things succumb.

The moonlight dances on the snow,
With each chill, the world will slow,
Painting white the earth below,
In this stillness, we shall grow.

Echoes fade, but memories stay,
In winter's heart, we find our way,
A timeless love, an ancient lore,
In the cold, we will explore.

Beneath the Weight of Winter's Touch

Beneath the weight of winter's grace,
A world transformed, a soft embrace,
Frozen rivers twist and flow,
Nature's hand, a gentle show.

Trees stand still, adorned in white,
Veils of snow, a shimmering sight,
As time drifts on in chilly air,
Moments lost without a care.

The chilling winds around us blow,
Through silent fields, where wild things go,
Each breath we take, a cloud of frost,
In winter's grasp, no warmth is lost.

A quiet strength beneath the snow,
Promises whispered, seeds to sow,
Life waits patient, hidden deep,
While winter sings its lullabies to keep.

The world awaits the thawing sun,
Underneath this weight, we run,
Through dreams that spark in icy air,
Beneath the weight, we find our care.

The Dreamer's Icebound Journey

Upon a path of glittered frost,
The dreamer's heart, though never lost,
Wanders through this frozen land,
Guided by a gentle hand.

Mountains whisper tales of old,
Of realms where dreams turn into gold,
With every step, the spirits soar,
In frozen dreams, we search for more.

The night unfolds, a canvas dark,
Stars alight, each a tiny spark,
In the quiet, echoes dance,
Inviting us to take a chance.

Across the snow, our visions glide,
In winter's chill, our hopes abide,
We find the warmth in icy gusts,
In dreams, we place our deepest trusts.

The journey ends where it began,
A circle drawn in natural span,
With frozen tales and dreams to share,
The dreamer's heart beats strong and rare.

Diamond Veils of Rest

In the twilight of a winter's sigh,
Diamond veils beneath the sky,
Softly falling, night's embrace,
A tranquil hush, a sacred space.

Stars, like jewels, twinkle bright,
Guardians of the cold, clear night,
While shadows stretch, they weave and drift,
In winter's lull, our spirits lift.

Beneath the moon, the world is still,
In diamond veils, our dreams we fill,
Each flake a wish, a whispered prayer,
In silent moments, we journey there.

The ground is soft, a tender bed,
Where thoughts take flight, and worries shed,
In peaceful dreams, we find our rest,
Wrapped in winter's gentle vest.

Tomorrow waits beyond the dawn,
In these veils, our hopes are drawn,
Through night's embrace, we find our way,
In diamond dreams, forever stay.

The Quiet Dance of Shimmering Shadows

In twilight's soft embrace, they sway,
Formed in whispers, fading away.
A gentle hush upon the ground,
While secret stories spin around.

Underneath the silver moon,
The shadows weave their silent tune.
With every flicker, they confide,
The beauty found when worlds collide.

A rustling breeze begins to play,
As night unfolds, soft dreams decay.
With shimmering light that bends and breaks,
The dance of shadows, the heart awakes.

They slip through cracks in time and space,
Unraveled tales, a timeless chase.
In their embrace, we find our place,
A quiet dance, a fleeting grace.

Lost in layers, shadows merge,
In this calm, a subtle surge.
With every heartbeat, we entrust,
The secrets held in morning's dust.

Polished Dreams in a Frozen Realm

In lands where time feels bittersweet,
The polished dreams beneath our feet.
Mirrored ice in glimmering hue,
Reflects the hopes of hearts so true.

Beneath the frost, the whispers dwell,
Of stories only ice can tell.
A breath of wind, a tale unfolds,
In frozen depths, a magic molds.

In every crystal, a vision gleams,
A world awash in silver streams.
From slumber's clutch, the dreams emerge,
In frozen realms, their spirits surge.

A dance of light on snowy plains,
Where joy and sorrow leave their stains.
The polished dreams that glisten bright,
Are boundless as the stars at night.

With every shimmer, hearts are freed,
In this realm where love takes heed.
We walk amidst the icy gleams,
Awakened now by polished dreams.

A Journey Through the Icy Veil

Through pathways wrapped in icy lace,
We tread softly, a sacred space.
A journey forged where silence reigns,
And hidden wonders call our names.

The crystalline air, its breath so pure,
Holds secrets deep that we must lure.
With every step, the world awakes,
Beneath the veil, where magic shakes.

In the shadows, echoes play,
Leading our minds, they softly say.
We wander through this fragile light,
In the embrace of endless night.

Each frost-kissed branch, a story speaks,
Of icy dreams and mystic peaks.
With hearts ablaze, we hold on tight,
To hope that shimmers, pure and bright.

As dawn breaks forth, the veil will lift,
Transforming all, a precious gift.
From icy depths to radiant skies,
We'll find our truth as daylight flies.

Crystalline Visions at Dawn

As dawn approaches, crystals gleam,
Awakening a slumbered dream.
The world adorned in silver light,
Where shadows dance to greet the bright.

Each facet catches morning's glow,
A symphony of frost and snow.
In visions vivid, colors blend,
While time unfolds, as moments mend.

The silence of the waking day,
Brings whispered winds that gently sway.
In each soft ray that breaks the dawn,
Crystalline visions, reborn and drawn.

Embracing warmth in nature's arms,
Where beauty's found in quiet charms.
A tapestry of life anew,
With every breath, the world rings true.

As sunlight spills on frozen ground,
In joyful whispers, life is found.
Crystalline hopes ride morning's sigh,
As dreams take flight to touch the sky.

Hidden Frost in Wandering Hearts

In shadows deep where silence reigns,
A lingering chill in hidden veins.
Whispers echo through the night,
Frosty breath in fleeting light.

Hearts that wander, lost and free,
Amidst the trees that sway with glee.
Each step taken, a story told,
In the frost where secrets unfold.

Beneath the stars, a soft embrace,
Time stands still in this sacred space.
The world outside fades far away,
As dreams and frost in stillness play.

Memories dance in the frozen air,
Stories shared without a care.
Echoes linger, soft and clear,
A tale of love, a ghostly sphere.

Awakening hearts in winter's grace,
Hidden frost, a warm embrace.
Through wandering paths, we find our way,
In the chill of night, forever stay.

Whispers of Winter's Veil

Soft and gentle, the snowflakes fall,
Covering earth in a silvery shawl.
Whispers swirl in the crisp night air,
Secrets carried, both fragile and rare.

Bare branches sway beneath the weight,
Of winter's touch, a quiet fate.
In the stillness, a heart beats slow,
Beneath the veil of white, we grow.

Fires crackle with stories untold,
Embers dance in shades of gold.
With every flicker, dreams ignite,
Casting shadows in the night's soft light.

Whispers linger, a haunting song,
In winter's arms, where we belong.
Nature's canvas, painted bright,
A symphony of warmth, despite the night.

In the silence, we find our peace,
Wrapped in winter's sweet release.
Underneath the stars so grand,
Whispers of love on frosted land.

Icy Echoes of Slumber

Sleepy town wrapped in a quilt,
Beneath the moon, where dreams are built.
Icy echoes through streets so still,
Every heart knows the winter's thrill.

Footsteps crunch on the snow-kissed ground,
In the night, a magic sound.
Crystals gleam in the pale moonlight,
Holding secrets, snug and tight.

Slumber creeps in, soft and slow,
As time dances in a gentle flow.
Wrapped in whispers, a tranquil tune,
As shadows play with the glowing moon.

In the stillness, a lullaby sings,
With every note, the heart takes wings.
Icy echoes weave a spell,
In the night, all is well.

Dreams take flight on winter's breeze,
Carried softly through the trees.
In this calm, we find our way,
Icy echoes of another day.

Chilled Reflections

The lake lies still, a mirror clear,
Reflecting skies both bright and near.
Chilled reflections dance in the night,
Framing moments, pure delight.

Each breath released in frosty air,
A moment captured, precious and rare.
Nature whispers in shimmers bright,
In the heart of winter's light.

The world slows down, the noise fades out,
Here in stillness, we learn to doubt.
What was said, and how it feels,
In chilled reflections, truth reveals.

Stars gaze down with watchful eyes,
Painting dreams across the skies.
In the quiet, we understand,
Chilled reflections throughout the land.

With every glance, a story shared,
In winter's grasp, we are prepared.
For the journey ahead, we embrace,
Chilled reflections, a loving grace.

Cold Caress of Morning Light

A whisper slides through frosty air,
The sun unfolds with tender care.
Its beams break through a silken haze,
Awakening the world to praise.

Each breath is crystal, echoes clear,
As daylight dances, bright yet near.
Soft kisses touch the frozen ground,
In this embrace, pure joy is found.

The trees stand tall with lace embraced,
In shimmering coats, their bark is graced.
Nature sighs in warmth's gentle glow,
A promise that spring soon will show.

A moment held, suspended high,
Where shadows play and dreams can fly.
The cold caress, a sweet surprise,
A hopeful heart beneath blue skies.

As light ascends, the chill subsides,
With every hue, the spirit glides.
In dawn's embrace, all life begins,
As morning blooms, our journey spins.

Fragments of Icicle Wishes

Hanging like dreams from rafters bright,
Icicles glisten, pure and light.
Each one a wish, a crystal tear,
Caught in time, it lingers near.

The wind whispers secrets, soft and low,
As winter's breath begins to flow.
Beneath their glint, a world asleep,
In frosted veils, promises keep.

Reflections beam in sapphire hues,
As daylight crosses dew-laden views.
Every shard a tale to tell,
Of fleeting moments, cast a spell.

With the sun's warmth, they start to fade,
Slipping away, this cool cascade.
Yet in their fall, hope's glow remains,
As springtime washes away the chains.

So collect these fragments, one by one,
Each drop a memory, softly spun.
For in their shimmer, dreams align,
A tapestry of wishes intertwined.

The Stillness of Shivered Imaginations

In twilight hours, when silence reigns,
Thoughts take flight on silver chains.
Quiet echoes through the night,
As shadows weave in gentle light.

Whispers float on frosted skies,
Imagination's wings arise.
They dance in dreams, both soft and bright,
Awakening the secret night.

Windows glow with warmth, a spark,
While outside geometry leaves its mark.
Each breath, a painting on the air,
A canvas stretched beyond despair.

In this stillness, worlds collide,
As visions blur with gentle pride.
The heart beats in a tender trance,
Yearning for each forgotten chance.

So linger here, where wonders bloom,
In shivered thoughts and whispered room.
For in the quiet, dreams align,
In stillness, hearts begin to shine.

Glistening Shadows at Dawn

The dawn awakens, shadows play,
A canvas painted in soft gray.
Colors spill in gentle floods,
As night retreats, the world now thuds.

Footsteps muffled by the frost,
In silence, we remember lost.
Glistening whispers touch the earth,
As day unfolds its vibrant birth.

Each ray a touch upon the skin,
Inviting warmth, enticing kin.
In every nook, light starts to grow,
While dreams released begin to flow.

Beneath the trees, shadows stretch wide,
Cloaked in hues where secrets hide.
Glistening trails on morning's face,
Marking paths of quiet grace.

So raise your eyes to the new day's song,
Where shadows know they can't be wrong.
With every breath, life sparks a fire,
In glistening light, our hearts aspire.

Flurries of Enigmatic Night

In the hush of dusk's gentle fold,
Whispers of secrets begin to unfold.
Stars peek through a quilt of gray,
As shadows dance and softly sway.

Fleeting moments drift through the air,
A tapestry woven with tender care.
Each flurry a note in the silent song,
A lullaby where dreams belong.

Moonlight glimmers on frost-kissed ground,
Mapping the silence with a soothing sound.
Here in the enclave of tranquil flight,
The world is reborn in mystical light.

Mysteries wrapped in a silvery shroud,
Echoes of wonder swirl unbowed.
Footprints vanish where wild thoughts roam,
In flurries of night, we find our home.

Hibernation's Gentle Embrace

Within the soft cradle of winter's chill,
Nature rests, obeying the still.
The earth sighs beneath a blanket white,
Cradled in solace, hidden from sight.

Silent moments stretch long and wide,
As hope takes refuge, dreams abide.
Beneath the frost, life takes a pause,
Wrapped in peace, without a cause.

Each flake that falls, a whisper made,
Blanketing earth in a soothing shade.
In this cocoon, all worries cease,
Hibernation grants a gentle peace.

Nature slumbers, time slows its race,
Held in the fold of winter's grace.
In the stillness, we all find space,
In hibernation's gentle embrace.

The Lattice of Chill and Wonder

Amidst the pines, where shadows play,
A lattice weaves through night and day.
Frosted whispers in branches sway,
Telling stories of skies turned gray.

Patterns form in a crystalline art,
Each flake unique, a fragile part.
In the hushed expanse of chilled air,
Nature's wonder spreads everywhere.

The glow of twilight, a delicate hue,
Unveils the magic in all that is new.
Under the moon's watchful eye,
The lattice of life, a breath, a sigh.

Veins of ice on glassy streams,
Reflecting the world of muted dreams.
Here in wonder, we pause and feel,
The lattice connects us, forever real.

Murmurs of a Snow-Kissed Slumber

In the quiet hours of the silver night,
Murmurs echo, soft and light.
Snowflakes drift like whispered vows,
Resting gently on sleeping boughs.

A lullaby borne from frosty air,
Tuning hearts in the stillness there.
Nature sighs, as if to say,
Dreams awaken with the break of day.

Shadows linger, cloaked in white,
Cradle the world in tranquil light.
A symphony of silence plays,
Guiding souls down winding ways.

Embers of warmth beneath the freeze,
The heart finds shelter with such ease.
In snow-kissed slumber, longing is found,
Among the whispers, love surrounds.

Mirage of Chilled Desires

In the stillness where shadows lie,
Frozen dreams drift and sigh,
Whispers linger like a ghost,
Yearning hearts, a haunted host.

Beneath the glaze of a distant moon,
Silent wishes fade too soon,
Fleeting glances of what could be,
Chilled desires, lost at sea.

Crystals dance on frosty breath,
Echoes softly tease of death,
Moments pass like fleeting grace,
In this mirage, an empty space.

Frosty fingers trace the air,
Caressing hopes, a whispered prayer,
Chasing visions, running wild,
Yet, in shadows, heart beguiled.

In the night, the secrets swell,
In solitude, they weave a spell,
A tapestry of truths and lies,
In a mirage where love never dies.

Glimmers in the Glistening Night

Stars cascade like drops of dew,
Lighting paths in shades so blue,
Twinkling jewels on endless sky,
Songs of night that subtly fly.

A hush envelops every street,
Softened shadows, cool and sweet,
Dreams awaken in the gloom,
Carried forth on winter's plume.

Moonlit whispers kiss the earth,
Painting memories, giving birth,
To echoes sounding through the trees,
A symphony on chilly breeze.

Every glow, a fleeting spark,
Guiding souls through ere the dark,
In the glow, the heart takes flight,
Glimmers dance in glistening night.

Silhouettes in silver gleam,
Life unfolds like tender dream,
Hope ignites with every breath,
In the magic of night's depth.

Threads of Cold and Light

Woven winds in twilight's loom,
Crafting tales of crisp perfume,
Cold and light in delicate dance,
Every glance a fleeting chance.

Frosty fingers touch the dawn,
Tracing paths that linger on,
Whispers echo through the chill,
As shadows linger, soft and still.

Sunlight breaks the icy veil,
Tales of warmth in winter's tale,
Threads entwined with every hue,
Moments bright, and hearts anew.

Crystalline patterns softly form,
In the quiet, find the warm,
Life is stitched with hope and dreams,
In the fabric, nothing seems.

In this world where cold holds sway,
Light will find its fervent way,
Binding hearts with every thread,
A canvas where our dreams are spread.

Smoky Whispers of Arctic Night

In the stillness, clove-scented haze,
Underneath the starlit gaze,
Voices lost in the vast expanse,
Smoky whispers weave their dance.

Frosty air embraces tight,
Cradling secrets of the night,
Ghostly trails in shadows creep,
Veiling dreams that never sleep.

Echoes rise from frozen ground,
Silent questions linger around,
In the chill, heartbeats align,
Seeking warmth from frost's design.

Beneath the cloak of drifting snow,
Silent stories begin to flow,
Embers glow in icy breath,
Life ignites amidst this death.

With every puff, the flames aspire,
Carving warmth from coldest fire,
In the dark, let hope ignite,
Through smoky whispers of the night.

Mirage of Winter's Soul

Silvery whispers dance with the cold,
Dreams of warmth are silently sold.
Frozen lakes reflect the pale moon,
Time stands still, a fleeting tune.

Winds weave tales of days gone by,
Underneath the heavy sky.
Nature rests in a soft embrace,
Hibernating in this tranquil space.

Branches bare, yet strong and bold,
Guarding secrets from the old.
Each flake falls, a gentle sigh,
A fleeting moment before it'll fly.

Beneath the frost, life waits and dreams,
In the silence, hope still gleams.
A mirage of warmth begins to swell,
Within winter's heart, I know it well.

The stillness speaks, a soft-spoken guide,
In this chilling world, love will abide.
As shadows linger and daylight wanes,
The soul of winter gently reigns.

A Tapestry of Snow-Laden Visions

Threads of silver weave through trees,
Whispers carry on the winters breeze.
Each flake, a note in nature's song,
Painting the earth where dreams belong.

Hushed tones blanket the world below,
Creating scenes in a far-off glow.
A tapestry stitched with care and grace,
In every corner, a warm embrace.

Frozen rivers flow in silent trance,
While shadows play in a snowy dance.
The night-time sky holds secrets tight,
A canvas painted with stars so bright.

Branches bend with burdens shared,
Nature's bounty, beautifully prepared.
Visions shimmer in the moon's soft light,
A fleeting glimpse of pure delight.

In this realm where silence reigns,
Every heartbeat echoes through the chains.
A tapestry that weaves the night,
Snow-laden dreams, a wondrous sight.

Chasing Shadows in the Frost

Morning breaks with a chill in the air,
Footprints follow where shadows stare.
Frosty whispers curl like smoke,
In this winter spell, hearts evoke.

Branches stretch, a skeletal frame,
As shadows flicker, wild and tame.
The frosted ground, a canvas white,
Invites the dance of day and night.

Silhouettes of trees loom overhead,
Echoes linger where dreams have fled.
Chasing whispers as they twirl and spin,
In the quiet, the chase begins.

Glistening trails of ice and snow,
Lead us through where soft winds blow.
With every step, the world feels new,
Chasing shadows that fade from view.

In the stillness, a world awakes,
Awakens joy in winter's stakes.
Together, we'll wander, hand in hand,
Chasing shadows in this frosty land.

Winter's Return to the Dreamscape

As whispers of winter brush the ground,
Dreams emerge where silence is found.
Crystalline sparkles ignite the air,
Awakening magic hidden with care.

The horizon blurs in a hazy mist,
Where echoes of dreams can't be dismissed.
Gentle snowflakes, a dreamer's touch,
In whispers of winter, we feel so much.

Moonlit nights in their tranquil glow,
Guide our hearts where the soft winds blow.
A return to the realms of our mind,
In winter's weave, true peace we find.

Gathering dreams like twinkling stars,
O'er the chill that whispers from afar.
Nature's embrace, a heavenly call,
In this dreamscape, we have it all.

With every breath, the world stands still,
Filling our hearts with winter's thrill.
A dance of dreams, both tender and true,
In winter's return, we find anew.

Threads of Ice in a Starlit Story

In the night, the stars align,
Whispers caught in frozen air.
Crystal threads, a tale divine,
Woven softly, dreams laid bare.

Frosted branches, shimmers glow,
Dance with echoes of the past.
Beneath the moon, a soft tableau,
Time stands still, a spell is cast.

Every flake, a story spun,
Glistening on the forest floor.
Nature's canvas, brightly done,
Through the night, we wander more.

In each shimmer, secrets sigh,
Tales of worlds we've yet to find.
Underneath the vast, dark sky,
Love and loss, forever bind.

As dawn breaks, the tales will fade,
Yet in hearts, the magic stays.
Threads of ice, in twilight made,
Sparkling in these starlit ways.

Winter's Softest Embrace

Snowflakes fall, a gentle brush,
Cloaking earth in silence sweet.
In the hush, all worries hush,
Winter's arms, a soft retreat.

Bare trees wear a crystal crown,
Rivers slow, a glassy sheen.
In this quiet, worry drowns,
Nature breathes, serene and clean.

Underneath a blank white sheet,
Dreams of spring begin to weave.
In the chill, warm hearts will meet,
Hope is sewn with every eve.

Each breath fogs the winter air,
Moments stitched with memory.
In the cold, we find a prayer,
Of togetherness, you and me.

As night falls, the stars will gleam,
Guiding us, a soft embrace.
In winter's arms, we dare to dream,
Finding warmth in this cold space.

Celestial Bodies in a Frosty Expanse

Stars above in velvet skies,
Twinkling like a thousand eyes.
Galaxies swirl, cosmic dance,
Frosty night, a timeless trance.

Comets streak with fiery tails,
Whispers of ancient, distant trails.
In the chill, we gaze and sigh,
Boundless dreams in the dark sky.

Planets spin in harmony,
Celestial whispers call to me.
Among the frost, I feel them near,
Secrets held, yet crystal clear.

Moonlit paths and shadows cast,
Remind us of the tales that passed.
In the night, a wish takes flight,
Through frozen time, we find our light.

As auroras dance in dawn's embrace,
Coloring skies with soft, warm grace.
Celestial bodies, in frosty cheer,
Guide our dreams throughout the year.

The Stillness of Frozen Reflections

In the pond, a mirror clear,
Stillness reigns, no sounds appear.
Frostbite kisses the gentle wave,
Nature's art, both wild and brave.

Over ice, the world holds breath,
Crystals gleam, a dance of death.
In the silence, stories grow,
Echoes of the chill below.

Glassy views of fleeting time,
Reflections caught in nature's rhyme.
Each ripple tells a tale of old,
Of secrets whispered, never told.

Winter's magic paints the scene,
With colors soft and evergreen.
In frozen peace, we feel the grace,
Of quiet hearts in nature's space.

As twilight deepens, shadows blend,
In the stillness, we transcend.
Frozen reflections softly call,
In their stillness, we find all.

A Chilled Embrace

In the frosty air we sit,
Wrapped in warmth, a gentle fit.
Whispers soft like falling snow,
In this stillness, love will grow.

Hands entwined, the world fades out,
Wrapped in silence, there's no doubt.
Each breath a cloud, a frosty sign,
Together here, our hearts align.

The night is deep, the stars will gleam,
In this winter's blissful dream.
In the cold, our spirits dance,
A timeless, sweet, enchanted chance.

Snowflakes kiss the windowpanes,
Melting worries, soothing pains.
A quiet joy in each embrace,
In the chill, we find our place.

As the night drifts into dawn,
Wrapped in warmth, the chill is gone.
In the morning light, we see,
Together in this harmony.

Crystal Tapestry of Thought

Thoughts like snowflakes drift and swirl,
Each one unique, a precious pearl.
Laced in frost, they softly gleam,
Crafting visions in a dream.

Weaving stories, colors bright,
In the hush of winter's night.
A tapestry, both vast and wide,
In this crystal world, we confide.

Every thread a memory spun,
Underneath the cold, pale sun.
Shimmering with each soft breath,
In this beauty, we find depth.

Anchored thoughts in icy streams,
Flowing gently, like our dreams.
Framed by silence, thoughts take flight,
In this winter's starry light.

With each echo, whispers play,
In a world of white and gray.
Carved by time, our minds entwine,
In this tapestry divine.

Snowbound Wishes

Under blankets, cozy tight,
Dreams dappled in soft white light.
Silent wishes, hearts laid bare,
In the snow, we find the flair.

Each flake a wish that takes its flight,
Carried softly through the night.
Whispers of hope on the breeze,
In the chill, our spirits ease.

Curling up by the fire's glow,
Counting all the dreams we sow.
Frosty windows, laughter shared,
In this moment, we're prepared.

Outside the world is dressed in white,
A landscape pure, a wondrous sight.
Snowbound wishes, gently flow,
In our hearts, the love will grow.

As morning breaks with a soft hue,
Every wish, a promise new.
In the snow, our dreams align,
Snowbound wishes, divine design.

The Silence of Frozen Fantasies

In the stillness, shadows creep,
Frozen fantasies, secrets keep.
Silent thoughts drift through the air,
In this moment, none compare.

Whispers echo, soft and light,
Dances of dreams in the night.
Frigid air, yet warm inside,
In this chill, our hopes abide.

Woven tales in twilight's glow,
Where the silent wonders flow.
Each breath a cloud, a fleeting song,
In frozen dreams, we all belong.

Cold embrace of winter's song,
In the silence, we grow strong.
Drifting softly, fantasies freeze,
In this moment, hearts find ease.

As dawn breaks, the fog will lift,
In the quiet, we find our gift.
The silence speaks, profound and clear,
In frozen fantasies, we're near.

The Art of Sleeping in Snow

Softly falls the blanket white,
Embracing all in gentle night.
Whispers weave 'neath moonlit gleam,
Nature sighs a silent dream.

Trees adorned in frosty lace,
Guard the quiet, sacred space.
Footfalls muffled, time stands still,
Echoes breathe in winter's chill.

Nestled in a world so pure,
Peaceful hearts, the snow's allure.
Slumber deep, let worries fade,
In this hush, all fears betrayed.

With each flake, a story told,
Innocence draped like fine gold.
Rest awaits, our spirits soar,
In the art of sleep, restore.

Morning glows with colors bright,
Awakens dreams from frozen night.
Yet the magic lingers on,
In the dance of dusk and dawn.

Winter's Serenade of Stillness

In the hush of winter's grace,
Nature wraps in soft embrace.
Snowflakes twirl like dancers free,
Whirling in a symphony.

Frosted branches gently sway,
Harmonizing night and day.
Stars above, like eyes so bright,
Gaze upon this tranquil sight.

Whispers carried on the breeze,
String of notes that gently tease.
Each breath hangs in frosty air,
A moment caught, beyond compare.

Silent nights where shadows creep,
Stories whispered, secrets deep.
In this world, the heart can mend,
Winter's song, a faithful friend.

Firelight crackles, warmth inside,
Reflecting on the world outside.
In the stillness, dreams ignite,
Becoming echoes of pure light.

Shrouded in Whispered Cold

Veils of silver cloak the land,
Nature's kiss, a gentle hand.
Every breath, a frozen spark,
Whispers linger in the dark.

Through the trees, the shadows play,
Twilight's hues in shades of gray.
Footsteps crunch on powdered ground,
Lost in time, nowhere found.

Moonlit trails invite to roam,
In this peace, we find our home.
Every flake a lullaby,
Each moment held, we cannot lie.

Wrapped in layers, hearts entwined,
In the cold, our spirits bind.
Nature's quilt, a soft embrace,
In whispered cold, we find our place.

Frosty windows, stories told,
Memories in winter's hold.
Here we linger, safe and sound,
In the cold, our love unbound.

Dreams Adrift on Icy Winds

Beneath the stars, a canvas wide,
Dreams take flight, as hearts collide.
Icy winds through branches weave,
Every sigh a chance to believe.

Snowflakes dance in swirling streams,
Carrying our deep-set dreams.
Gentle whispers call us near,
In this chill, our hopes are clear.

Wrapped in warmth, we face the night,
Chasing shadows, finding light.
Frozen fantasies take flight,
In the crispness, pure delight.

With each gust, the world feels new,
Painting skies in shades of blue.
Letting go of all that weighs,
In the snow, our worries graze.

As dawn breaks with golden hue,
We awaken to a world anew.
Dreams adrift on icy breath,
In nature's grace, we conquer death.

Chill of the Luminous Dreamscape

In twilight's soft embrace, we wander,
Through whispers of the night, growing fonder.
Stars alight like silver keys,
Unlocking secrets in the breeze.

A canvas blank, with shades of blue,
Each stroke a memory, pure and true.
Floating softly, dreams take flight,
Carried gently by the night.

The moon casts shadows, rich and deep,
While crickets sing the songs of sleep.
A tapestry of shimmering hues,
Binds our hearts to evening's muse.

In stillness, time begins to pause,
Nature's wonders, endless cause.
The chill enchants, it calls our name,
Within its warmth, we'll never wane.

So let us drift on waves of light,
In dreamscape's embrace, till the dawn's sight.
With every pulse, we feel the beat,
A luminous chill, our hearts will greet.

Icy Rhapsody of the Soul

In frozen realms where silence reigns,
The music of the night remains.
Each snowflake dances, pure and bright,
A serenade in dazzling white.

The world transformed, a crystal sphere,
Echoes of beauty draw us near.
With every breath, the chill is sweet,
An icy rhapsody, soft and fleet.

The moonlight glimmers on the frost,
In the quietude, we are lost.
Whispers of winter fill the air,
Inviting dreams as we share.

Among the pines, the shadows play,
With melodies that sway and sway.
Nature hums a soothing tune,
Underneath the watchful moon.

In this embrace of chill divine,
Our souls entwine through icy wine.
Sipping slowly, we'll taste the night,
With rhapsodies that freeze in flight.

The Slumbering Heart of Winter

Beneath the snow, the world sleeps still,
The heart of winter, calm and chill.
Wrapped in blankets, soft and white,
A slumbering dream, devoid of light.

Each breath a cloud, a fleeting ghost,
In this season, we cherish most.
The branches bow beneath the weight,
Of soft enchantments, oh so great.

Time drips slowly, a frozen stream,
Silhouettes dance in midnight's dream.
The quiet hum of nature's song,
Whispers secrets to us long.

The frost-kissed air, so crisp and pure,
Invites our hearts to yet endure.
We find a warmth in chilly nights,
In winter's grip, our spirit ignites.

As slumber holds the silent ground,
In the stillness, hope is found.
The heart of winter beats so slow,
Reviving life from depths below.

Flickers of Light in a Shattered Freeze

Amidst the cold, where shadows creep,
Flickers of light begin to leap.
With each glimmer, hope ignites,
Transforming dark into delights.

The ice may shatter, crisp and clear,
Yet warmth dances, drawing near.
These twinkling sparks, so bright and bold,
Speak of stories yet untold.

Through winter's grasp, we find our way,
Light blooms gently, day by day.
Hearts entwined in the frozen breath,
Embrace the magic, conquer death.

In fractured glass, reflections gleam,
Capturing fragments, a waking dream.
The chill persists, yet warmth will rise,
Flickers of light under vast skies.

So let us gather, hand in hand,
In the frozen tapestry, we stand.
Together we shine, through darkened seas,
Flickers of hope in shattered freeze.

Glacial Reveries

In silence, icebergs drift afar,
Whispers of dreams beneath the star.
Hues of blue in a world so still,
Time's embrace brings a gentle thrill.

Frosted landscapes stretch and sway,
Memories linger, come what may.
Each flake dances in moonlit grace,
A tranquil heart finds its rightful place.

Frozen lakes reflect the night,
Mirrors of memories, pure and bright.
Nature's quilt, a chilly embrace,
In the depths, I find my space.

The winds carry tales of old,
Stories of warmth in the bitter cold.
Echoes of laughter, soft and sweet,
In this realm, my soul finds its seat.

Through glacial reveries, we glide,
In this dreamscape, nowhere to hide.
With whispered wishes wrapped in ice,
We wander, lost but feeling nice.

Crystal-Cloaked Fantasies

Beneath the shimmer of frost-kissed nights,
A world of wonder, gleaming with lights.
Crystal cloaks drape the sleeping earth,
Holding secrets of magic and mirth.

Glistening paths adorned with white,
Each step echoes in the soft moonlight.
Frosty whispers caress the air,
Awakening dreams, soft and rare.

In this fantasy where shadows play,
Every heartbeat finds its way.
The silver stars wink above,
Reminding us all of forgotten love.

Icicles hanging, sharp and bold,
Stories of warmth, waiting to be told.
In this moment, we dance and spin,
In crystal dreams, our new lives begin.

Each breath turns to mist in the cold,
Embracing the magic, a sight to behold.
In crystal-cloaked fantasies, we find,
The light of hope forever entwined.

Sleep Beneath a Frozen Sky

Stars blanket the sky in silent repose,
As the world slumbers, wrapped in its clothes.
Underneath, secrets of winter hide,
While dreams take flight on the chill of the tide.

Snowflakes whisper lullabies sweet,
Carrying wishes on the soft winter beat.
In the dark, the heart finds its glowing thread,
Awakening stories where silence has led.

Frozen branches cradle the light,
As dusk gives way to the starry night.
In this hush, the soul finds its gear,
In the frosty air, we have nothing to fear.

Each star a promise, bright and bold,
In the freeze, warmth does unfold.
Sleep caresses the earth so deep,
In slumber's embrace, our dreams we keep.

Beneath the frozen sky, we lay,
Wrapped in night's gentle array.
With twinkling eyes and hearts that sigh,
We find our peace as we drift and lie.

Shimmers of Frostbitten Hope

In the early dawn, frost gleams bright,
Casting jewels in the soft daylight.
Each shimmer whispers of promise near,
That hope remains even through fear.

Biting winds sing a chilling tune,
Yet within blooms warmth under the moon.
Amidst the cold, tenacity glows,
Nurtured by the heart's vibrant throes.

Every flake that falls brings a new chance,
A reminder to life, a spirited dance.
Hope flickers softly in the chill of the air,
A beacon of light in a world so rare.

Icicles dangle, a sharpness that gleams,
Yet within their edges lie beautiful dreams.
These whispers of frostbite, though cold,
Are treasures of warmth, stories untold.

In each breath of winter, we find our way,
Shimmers of hope guide us through gray.
Together we rise, facing the fight,
With frostbitten hearts igniting the light.

Radiance in a Casket of Snow

In the stillness where silence lies,
The snowflakes dance and softly sigh.
A glimmer bright beneath the cold,
Whispers of warmth, a story told.

Each flake a gem, so pure, so bright,
A treasure forged in the dark of night.
Crystals twinkle, a frozen glow,
Embracing all in the casket of snow.

Winds carry tales through the pines,
Nature's breath, where beauty shines.
Amidst the chill, a heart still beats,
Finding solace where snow conceits.

Tracks of creatures, brief and light,
Mark the passage, a fleeting sight.
In every drift, a world so fair,
A canvas white, a dream laid bare.

As twilight whispers its gentle tune,
Stars emerge, a silver swoon.
In the quiet, love may glow,
Radiant hearts in a casket of snow.

The Melody of Ice and Light

In winter's grasp, a symphony plays,
Where ice and light weave through the days.
Each note a sparkle, each chord a climb,
Echoes of frost in a timeless rhyme.

Beneath the surface, a world concealed,
Secrets of silence, slowly revealed.
In shimmering hues, the night ignites,
The melody of ice and lights.

A crystal flute, the breeze takes flight,
Through branches bare, the stars ignite.
Harmony sings in the chilly air,
Nature's hands crafting joys to share.

Footsteps crunch on paths of white,
Each sound a note, a pure delight.
In every breath, a wonder finds,
The melody of ice that binds.

As dawn awakens, the colors blend,
A symphony that will never end.
In twilight's glow, hearts take their flight,
To the rhythm of ice and light.

Reflections in a Shivering Pond

Amidst the trees where shadows dance,
A pond lies still, a frozen trance.
Mirrored skies of silver hue,
Whisper secrets, old and new.

In every ripple, memories glow,
Reflections flicker in the cold below.
Time stands still in this quiet realm,
Nature's beauty at the helm.

Frost-kissed edges, a fragile thread,
Where dreams float lightly, softly spread.
Beneath the ice, life waits to wake,
In silence deep, the hearts may quake.

Crisp air carries a haunting call,
Winter's touch envelops all.
In every glance, a moment holds,
Reflections glimmer, stories told.

As twilight descends, shadows blend,
The pond's embrace, where visions mend.
A canvas drawn in the evening's song,
Reflections linger, where hearts belong.

Winter's Dreamscape Unveiled

In the hush of dawn, the world unwinds,
A tapestry woven with frost entwined.
Each branch a story, elegantly told,
In winter's dreamscape, a wonder bold.

Clouds drift softly, painting the sky,
The breath of winter, a whispered sigh.
Footprints fade in the shimmering white,
Carving paths through the gentle light.

Stars linger long in the morning glow,
Where secrets of night softly flow.
Each moment a treasure, a fleeting glance,
In winter's fabric, a timeless dance.

Snowflakes whisper from heaven's gate,
Wrapping the world in a gentle weight.
In the stillness, hearts start to gleam,
A magic born from a winter dream.

As day unfolds, shadows entwine,
In nature's arms, the beauty shines.
With every breath, the spirit feels,
Winter's dreamscape, a world revealed.

The Stillness of Frosted Memories

In winter's hush, silence grows,
Soft whispers dance where no one goes.
Shadows linger, veiled in white,
Frosted dreams in the pale moonlight.

Time stands still, as echoes fade,
Memories trapped, in ice they wade.
Each breath a puff, through chilly air,
Frigid moments we used to share.

Glistening thoughts, like crystals laid,
Fragile fragments, never swayed.
In the stillness, hearts ignite,
Frosted memories, warm and bright.

Underneath the canopy's gleam,
Lies a world wrapped in a dream.
Beneath the frost, stories weave,
In this stillness, we believe.

As daylight breaks, shadows break free,
Frosted memories, calling me.
In gentle warmth, we find our way,
Through stillness born from yesterday.

In the Heart of the Crystal Night

Stars are scattered, diamond-like,
In the heart of the crystal night.
Whispers linger on the breeze,
Carried softly through the trees.

Moonlight dances on the snow,
Painting paths where dreams can flow.
Each step echoes, a fleeting sound,
In this stillness, peace is found.

The world is hushed, wrapped in grace,
Time slows down in this embrace.
Hearts entwined beneath the glow,
In the night where feelings grow.

Frosted breath, a fleeting sigh,
Moments shared beneath the sky.
In the heart, where love takes flight,
Cradled close in the crystal night.

As dawn approaches, shadows blend,
In the heart, where dreams transcend.
Whispers linger, hope ignites,
Shining bright in the crystal nights.

Slumbering Beneath the Icy Canopy

Beneath the trees, a hush descends,
A frozen world where winter bends.
Softly wrapped in blankets white,
Slumbering dreams in the quiet night.

Branches laden, heavy with snow,
Whispers echo, muffled and slow.
In this stillness, time drifts away,
The icy canopy holds its sway.

Stored away, memories lie,
Beneath the frost, where silence sighs.
Hearts that wander through the cold,
Find warmth in stories yet untold.

In gentle peace, we close our eyes,
Where the frozen whispers arise.
Slumber deep, beneath the sky,
In the embrace of night's soft sigh.

Awake we'll find, when spring is near,
The dreams we held, crystal clear.
But for now, in white we stay,
Slumbering beneath the cold display.

Frozen Melodies of the Heart

In the quiet, melodies play,
Notes are frozen, drift away.
Capturing whispers, soft and sweet,
In the heart where shadows meet.

Echoes carved in winter's chill,
Fill the air, a haunting thrill.
Strings of silver, gentle sighs,
Frozen songs beneath the skies.

Chords of memories softly ring,
Frosted feelings, the heart takes wing.
In the stillness, love's refrain,
Melodies linger, like gentle rain.

Fingers trace the icy notes,
In this world where stillness floats.
With every breath, the music starts,
Frozen melodies touch our hearts.

As the dawn breaks, warm and clear,
The frozen songs, we hold them near.
In golden light, we find our part,
Singing frozen melodies of the heart.

Echoes of the Winter Sky

Whispers ride the chilly breeze,
Stars hide behind the twilight trees.
Softly, the snow begins to fall,
Nature wraps us in its thrall.

Echoes dance in frosted air,
Memories of warmth linger there.
Moonlight glistens on the white,
Illuminating the quiet night.

Pine branches bow beneath the weight,
Silence reigns, a spell so great.
In the quiet, time stands still,
Winter's magic bends our will.

Footsteps crunch on the snow below,
Each sound soft, like whispered flow.
We breathe in the crisp, cold air,
Lost in thoughts, without a care.

The sky wears a cloak of gray,
Yet joy in our hearts will stay.
As the day fades into dreams,
Hope warms us with gentle beams.

Tempest of Snowflakes

A flurry swirls, a dance untamed,
Among the forest, wild and framed.
Snowflakes waltz in the chill night,
Shimmering like diamonds in flight.

Each crystal spins, a tale to tell,
Of winter's breath, a magic spell.
Whirling winds rise to a hum,
A symphony of winter's drum.

Echoing through the frozen land,
Softly, the night makes its stand.
Footprints lost in the falling white,
As shadows dance in fading light.

The tempest stirs with icy breath,
Holding secrets of life and death.
In the storm, we find our peace,
As wild whispers never cease.

Nature's fury, fierce and bold,
In its embrace, our worries fold.
For in the chaos, beauty lies,
Underneath the stormy skies.

A world transformed, serene and still,
Carried on winter's gentle will.
Each moment a fleeting grace,
In the tempest's soft embrace.

Secrets Cradled in Frosted Silence

A blanket drapes the sleeping earth,
Guarding secrets of its worth.
Frosted whispers kiss the ground,
In their quiet, truth is found.

Branches bow with snowy weight,
Hiding tales of love and fate.
In the stillness, we can hear,
Silent stories drawing near.

Shimmering shards of ice and light,
Glimmering like stars at night.
In shadows cast by candle glow,
A glow of warmth begins to grow.

Time slows down in wintry grasp,
Life's precious moments held to clasp.
Beyond the veil of frost and cold,
Lies a beauty to behold.

In twinkling frost, our hearts align,
Lingering dreams in a bracing time.
Cradled softly in frozen breath,
Secrets bloom in winter's depth.

The Constellation of Frozen Thoughts

Stars of winter dot the night,
Each one whispers soft delight.
Frozen thoughts like icy streams,
Flow through the heart as fleeting dreams.

In the stillness, musings flow,
As snowflakes dance in moon's soft glow.
Each thought a spark, a shining thread,
Woven through the night, widespread.

Constellations of hopes and fears,
Glitter dazzling, washed in tears.
Hearts entwined in the chill's embrace,
Finding warmth in a cold place.

With every breath, nostalgia blooms,
A language spoken in silent rooms.
Moments frozen, yet alive,
In this space, our dreams survive.

As dawn approaches, skies will clear,
The constellations disappear.
But in our souls, they ever gleam,
Guiding us like a cherished dream.

A tapestry of softest snow,
Awakening the heart's own glow.
In the quiet depths of night,
Frozen thoughts take wing in flight.

The Frozen Palette of Imagination

A canvas waits, so stark and white,
Colors hide, yet yearn for light.
Brush in hand, the dreams ignite,
Each stroke whispers through the night.

Frosted hues of blue and gold,
Stories waiting to be told.
Shadows dance where thoughts unfold,
In this realm, the brave and bold.

Chill of winter, warm of heart,
Crafting worlds, a work of art.
With every shade, a brand new start,
The frozen dreams, a timeless part.

Vivid landscapes, skies of gray,
Painting hope in disarray.
Every vision finds its way,
On this palette, bright and fey.

Imagination's frosty flight,
Glitters softly in the night.
A dance of colors, pure delight,
Within the frozen, feels so right.

Ethereal Frostbites of Thought

Whispers linger in the air,
Thoughts like snowflakes, rare and fair.
Each one melts without a care,
Ethereal frost bites everywhere.

In the silence, ideas bloom,
Breath of winter, dispels the gloom.
A fleeting dance, a spark of room,
In the cold, the mind finds womb.

Crisp reflections, sharp and clear,
Echoes of what we hold dear.
In the frost, there lies no fear,
Only visions that draw near.

Thoughts suspended, still they glide,
With the chill they gently ride.
In the stillness, dreams abide,
Ethereal frost where hopes reside.

Fractured light through icy panes,
Capturing hopes and hidden pains.
Beneath the frost, the heart still gains,
Ethereal whispers break the chains.

Hushed Pathways in the Snow

Footsteps crunch on powdered white,
Paths unwritten in the night.
Silent journeys, pure delight,
Hushed pathways, dreams take flight.

Beneath the stars, the world asleep,
Among the pines, secrets keep.
In the frost, the spirits leap,
In every drift, the heart will weep.

Trails of wonder, softly laid,
In the silence, promises made.
Through the shadows, memories played,
In this hush, our fears allayed.

Magic lingers, cold embrace,
Each breath forms a crystal trace.
Through the veil, we find our place,
Hushed pathways weave a gentle grace.

As dawn approaches, light will show,
The beauty in the falling snow.
In our hearts, we come to know,
Hushed pathways are where dreams grow.

Suspended between Chill and Warmth

Morning breaks with soft sunlight,
Chill of dawn yields to warmth's light.
Frost and fire share respite,
Suspended moments, pure delight.

In the gaps, our breaths converge,
Warmth of hope begins to surge.
Through the cold, our hearts emerge,
Suspended pulse, a subtle urge.

Hands entwined, a quiet grace,
In between, we find our space.
Chill and warmth in sweet embrace,
Suspended here, we trace our place.

Winter's chill, yet embers glow,
Through the frost, our feelings flow.
In this balance, love will grow,
Suspended moments, heartbeats know.

As twilight drops, the day will end,
Chill of night, to warmth, we blend.
In this world, our souls transcend,
Suspended dreams that we defend.

Milton Keynes UK
Ingram Content Group UK Ltd.
UKHW010230111224
452348UK00011B/639